# BERMUDA

South Shore

# BERMUDA

## SCOTT STALLARD

OAKWELL
BOULTON

THIS BOOK IS DEDICATED TO MY FAMILY

Copyright © 1989 Boulton Publishing Services Inc.,
Toronto
Photographs © Scott Stallard, Bermuda
Designed by Sheena McKenzie, Toronto
Produced by the Oakwell Press,
a division of Boulton Publishing Services Inc.
ISBN 0-920831-10-9

Printed and bound in Hong Kong by Book Art Inc.,
Toronto

Distributed in Canada by
McClelland and Stewart, Inc., Toronto
Distributed in the United States by
Independent Publishers Group, Chicago

# ACKNOWLEDGEMENTS

This book represents over three years of photographing Bermuda. During that time, a number of people contributed to its formation in a variety of ways. I would like therefore to express my sincere thanks to the following persons for their valuable assistance in helping me to fulfil one of my goals.

The unfailing support from my parents Margaret and Sidney Stallard, and sister Nancy, has immeasurably encouraged this endeavour.

Teddy and Edna Tucker, whose concern for life in and around Bermuda makes it an honour to have them so closely associated with the book.

Robert Stigwood, my former employer, who allowed me time and opportunity to pursue my photography and cultivate a strong artistic sense.

Jodi De Crenza, William Kempe and Charlotte Walker for their numerous trips with my slides to Ken Lieberman Labs in New York. Robert and Gail Henderson and Nick Baldwin, who acted as my sounding board while editing, Carolyn Mello, Neil Bonin, Kerry Whittaker and Mike Spurling, whose avid interest in my work fuelled my determination. Wendell Hollis for his help with captioning information and Ann Spurling for technical advice.

Further support has come from "Stockphotos" in New York City, my stock agent, and Maryellen Ford of Ford Models in New York, whose encouragement led to my gaining representation there.

To Sheena McKenzie for her expertise with the layout and design, and Margaret Potts for her helpful advice on all aspects of the project.

A special thank you to Roger Boulton for all his work on the book and for having faith enough to publish it. To the Boulton family for their "Bermuda style" hospitality while accommodating me in Toronto.

Finally a "thank you" to Bermuda and to the people of the Island, who are dedicated to preserving that beauty which compels us to capture it on film.

SCOTT STALLARD
St George, Bermuda

House signs framed in hibiscus

# AUTHOR'S PREFACE

Waking up to the kind of peace that few countries know, whether it be raining or one of those glorious balmy days. Clean crisp air with the bonus of an occasional flowery fragrance. The sight of a bluebird nesting, or the longtails in April. Fry leaping on a calm day, and transparent water tinted all shades of blue.

The quality of life in Bermuda.

If there is one theme that runs through the photographs in this book, it is simply the quality of our environment. Conspicuous by their absence are the satellite dishes, telephone poles and wires, high-density housing, and streets congested with traffic.

Responsibility for our surroundings lies with every member of our society. It is partly the intention of this book to raise awareness toward preserving that which has taken centuries of hard work and respect for the land and sea and all that depend upon them.

To save some endangered species we resort to placing them in zoos and reserves. Let us ensure that in the coming years our environmental heritage will not be found only in the pages of a photographic book.

SCOTT STALLARD
St George, Bermuda

# INTRODUCTION

To look through this book is to view Bermuda's past and present, examined in great detail by a young man of artistic and photographic ability. The natural beauty as well as the accomplishments of Bermuda's architects are admirably presented in examples of the homes and in the coverage of Bermuda's two town centres, Hamilton and St George.

Scott Stallard has the skill it takes to capture this natural beauty on film, through informative and educational photography. His pictorial essay is of the highest quality. His book examines the style of life in these Islands and the thoughts behind the development of their resources throughout the years.

Bermuda is like a small ship in the middle of a huge ocean. Six hundred miles from the closest land, it requires managing with the greatest care and thought. Situated on the southern perimeter of a drowned volcano, surrounded by the Atlantic Ocean, which is over two miles deep in this geographical area, Bermuda is the most northern location where coral grows, and is also a home for many species of subtropical fish and crustaceans that inhabit the regions far to the south. In the past, sea turtles laid their eggs on Bermuda's beaches, and migratory birds wintered here. From historical records we know that Bermuda was the year-round home of the great whales and that the seas were full of great fishes.

"The land was all over with flowers, the air was filled with fowl beyond count, and the sea was with fish like no man has seen!" This quotation was taken from the account of a survivor of the wreck of two Spanish ships lost on the west reefs in 1639.

Today, unfortunately, the fish have nearly disappeared, the migratory birds are gone, the sea turtles are temporary visitors, and the humpback whales bypass Bermuda on their migration from the Banks to the south of the Island of Hispaniola to their feeding grounds off New England and Nova Scotia. Man has most certainly made serious incursions into the environment, which have in turn upset the natural

The photographs depicted in this book capture past accomplishments in architecture and building for the small community that inhabited Bermuda. The economy consisted of farming, fishing, tourism and servicing the navy and military required to support the British colonies in the Western Hemisphere. This phase of Bermuda's development lasted from the mid-18th century until after World War II, when the tourism industry took off with tremendous energy, followed in the late 1950's by the start of the offshore banking and insurance business. This was the beginning of the rapid decline in Bermuda's environment—too much concrete, too many people, too many motor cars. This situation has led to a decline in Bermuda's attractiveness to both visitors and local inhabitants, human and animal alike.

With his photographs, Scott Stallard has made a great contribution, and without a doubt has captured the beauty of Bermuda in this spectacular book. Such pictorial splendour, depicting man's impact on a small island, has not been accomplished before in recent times.

This collection of photographs touches on the concerns regarding the environment, and for the Bermuda that we are doing our utmost to protect and preserve for the future.

TEDDY TUCKER

**TEDDY TUCKER**—world-renowned treasure-diver, film-advisor, lecturer, conservationist and raconteur extraordinaire. A Bermudian descended from the Tucker family who arrived in Bermuda early in the seventeenth century, Teddy has been diving most of his life. He is a member of most of the world's diving societies and museums, is a longtime member of the Explorers' Club and has been associated with *National Geographic* for many years. In addition he has been a consultant to the Smithsonian Institution.

Teddy is a well-loved and respected member of the Bermuda community. He is also a colourful and fascinating personality, with a wealth of knowledge about the island home he loves so much. He was a "conservationist" long before the word came into constant use, and is an outspoken champion of Bermuda's environmental preservation.

Approaching Bermuda from the northwest at 30,000 feet

Mid Afternoon, Mid Ocean

Desmond Fountain's bronze tribute to Sir George Somers, his arms raised to the heavens, in thanks for having survived the tempest and shipwreck of 1609

Gable-end and buttery roofs; the unique style of Bermudian architecture

An old rough cedar gate, Bailey's Bay

Donkey-beetle on the style of a hibiscus

Forty years after the blight, dead cedars still await regeneration, although a number of cedars on Wreck Hill in Sandys have come back to life

Red oleander and a deep blue Bermuda sky

Replica of the *Deliverance* on Ordnance Island, St George; a project coordinated by the
Junior Service League. The original ship was built between 1609 and 1610 from the wreck
of the *Sea Venture* and sailed on to Jamestown, Virginia, with the *Patience*, carrying 130 people

Bermuda oranges catch the midmorning sun

The quaint old cobbler's shop window, Kent Street, St George

Relics from days gone by. . . .

Printer's Alley, St George.

August bikinis, South Shore, St George

Looking east along South Shore, toward Mid Ocean Beach, St George's

Pink oleander adorns a wall, Keith Hall Road, Warwick



Kathy Madeiros takes "Consider It Done" over the jumps at the Spicelands Riding Centre, Warwick

Little girl enjoying the annual Cup Match festivities at St George on the first day of August

Cup Match umbrellas keep the heat off spectators

Captivated by cricket

Six runs for St George in the Cup Match. In this annual two-day cricket match a team from St George plays a team from Somerset for the coveted trophy

Clean bowled! Cup Match action

Bridge House, King Street, St George. Built between 1690 and 1700, this was the home of some of the early Governors and prominent merchants

The Bermuda Aquarium fishing boat, facing Flatts Inlet. Originally ketch-rigged, the *Iridio* has been in continuous service for sixty years

A Bermuda roof gets a new coat of whitewash

Typical Bermuda roof and chimney at Owl's Cliff, Harrington Sound, Smith's

The boathouse and the bay, at Blue Horizons, Tucker's Town

Shallow sandy waters of Tucker's Town Bay

Blighted cedars take root in the blue sky

Gibb's Hill Lighthouse, atop Lighthouse Hill. Built in 1846 of cast iron, the structure stands 117 feet tall on a hill 239 feet above sea level. The beacon has been seen by ships as far as 40 miles away

Horses and carriage on South Road, overlooking Horseshoe Bay, Southampton

An old cannon on Ordnance Island points toward Penno's Wharf, St George

The magnificent Bermuda Easter lily. Each year at Easter time a gift of lilies is sent to Queen Elizabeth II by the people of Bermuda

Converging lines of the pathway to St James's Church in Sandys Parish

A proud father greets his daughter as she arrives at the church by carriage on her wedding day

The bride and her bridesmaids proceed to St James's Church

Wreck House, Wreck Hill Estate, Sandys

A West End pool is framed by Norfolk pines

Quarried limestone blocks await the mason

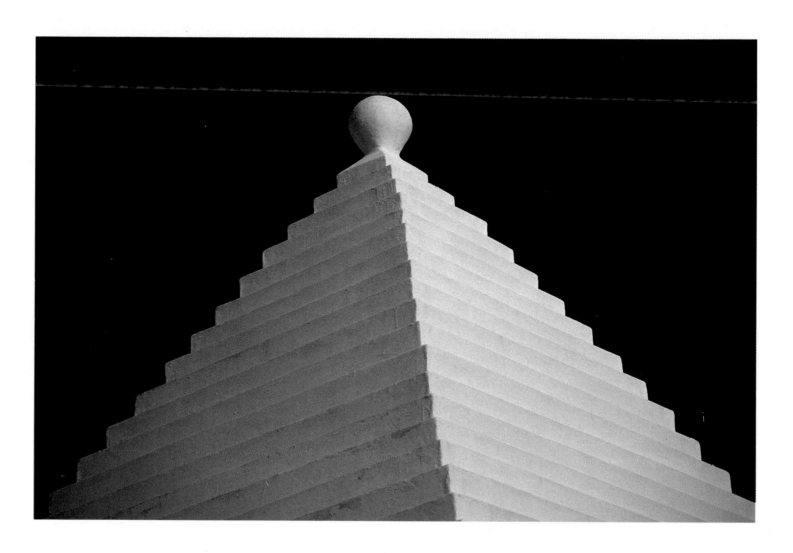

Buttery roof, The Buttery, Wellington Park, St George

The home of Joseph Stockdale, who brought the first printing press to Bermuda in 1783 and founded the *Bermuda Gazette*

Red sage lantana; the berries of this plant are a source of food for many birds

The Union Jack flutters in the northwesterly breeze on a crisp winter day at Ely's Harbour, Sandys

Billowing cloud formations above a boathouse, Sandys

War veterans, at eleven o'clock on the morning of 11 November, Remembrance Day

The Bank of N.T. Butterfield, with replicas of the stocks and pillory in  front, King's Square, St George

The *Jezebel*, a classic motor yacht of the 1930s, alongside No. 6 Dock, City of Hamilton

Members of the Bermuda Parliament, in top hats and tails, leaving the Sessions House on the occasion of the opening of Parliament

Wide view from Gibb's Hill Lighthouse looking to the northeast

View from Gibb's Hill Lighthouse, towards Perot's Island and Riddell's Bay

Bait fisherman looking for fry, Wreck Bay, Sandys

The oldest pedal cycle of its type in Bermuda, originally owned by
Sarah Hayward Smith, the first Matron of the Cottage Hospital

The casuarina cone—a menace to small children with bare feet!

Racing yachts moored together at the Royal Hamilton Amateur Dinghy Club, after the Newport-to-Bermuda race

Early bicycles had license plates (see previous page)

A windsurfer is bathed in the orange light of the sun

Front Street shops, Trimingham's, Smith's and Gosling's, City of Hamilton

Horse and buggy on Lighthouse Hill, Southampton

A tranquil lane in Somerset, shaded by cedars and Spanish moss

Front Street shops, Trimingham's, Smith's and Gosling's, City of Hamilton

Horse and buggy on Lighthouse Hill, Southampton

A tranquil lane in Somerset, shaded by cedars and Spanish moss

Vivid green avocados ripen in the sun

Under the beach umbrella, Windsor Beach, Tucker's Town

Derelict buildings near Lover's Lake, Ferry Reach, St George's

Honey-bee gathering nectar from the blossom of a citrus tree

The tranquil waters of Ely's Harbour, Sandys

Bermuda stone chimney, all that remains of a house that looked out across Shelly Bay

St Peter's Church, oldest Anglican church still in use in the western hemisphere. Built in 1612, it contains a fine abundance of ancient cedar work

Bright yellow allamanda

The tranquil waters of Ely's Harbour, Sandys

Bermuda stone chimney, all that remains of a house that looked out across Shelly Bay

St Peter's Church, oldest Anglican church still in use in the western hemisphere. Built in 1612, it contains a fine abundance of ancient cedar work

Bright yellow allamanda

The guest cottage, formerly a slave kitchen, *circa* 1815, at Sandymount, Bailey's Bay,  Hamilton

The unfinished church, Church Folly Lane, St George; work on this church began in 1870, to replace St Peter's, but disputes arose during construction and the work was never completed

Fishing nets and fishing boat, Flatts Inlet, Flatts Village, Smiths

Young boy chasing mullet in Tucker's Town Bay

A roadside cottage in Mullet Bay, St George. Pink is a popular colour for houses in Bermuda

Willoughby, overlooking Bailey's Bay and Bay Island, on Fractious Street, Hamilton Parish

A tunnel of trees shades South Road alongside the Botanical Gardens, Paget

Famous for its fishing tradition, St David's Island still offers the best fish chowder in Bermuda

Dredging for mussels, Harrington Sound, Hamilton

Harbourside home and yacht, St George Harbour

The Somerset ferry passes Lantana Cottages on its way back to the City of Hamilton

An old birdhouse sits atop a dead cedar, surrounded by bougainvillea

"Read me a Story"; these bronze statues by Desmond Fountain add to the charm of the gardens of Lantana Cottages in Somerset

An old birdhouse sits atop a dead cedar, surrounded by bougainvillea

"Read me a Story"; these bronze statues by Desmond Fountain add to the charm of the gardens of Lantana Cottages in Somerset

Seed of the pandanus tree, known locally as the screw pine

Dawn light over Mullet Bay, St George

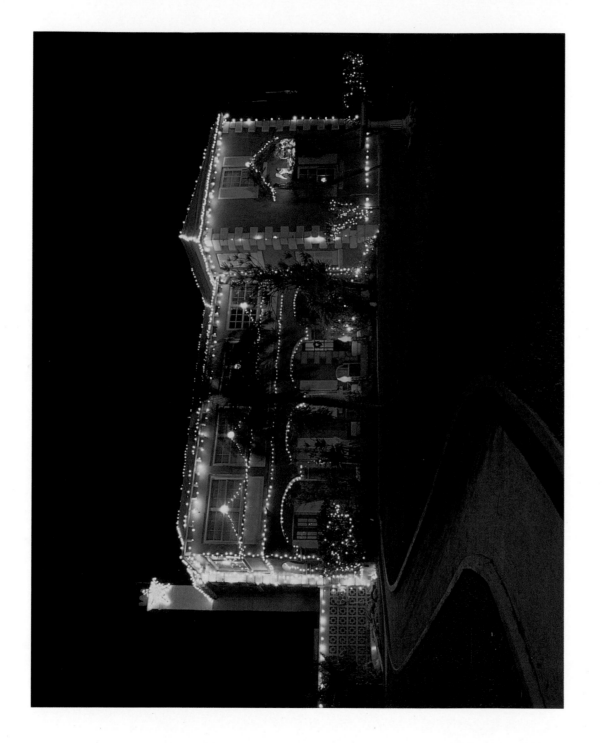

A home on Cavendish Road, magnificently decorated for Christmas

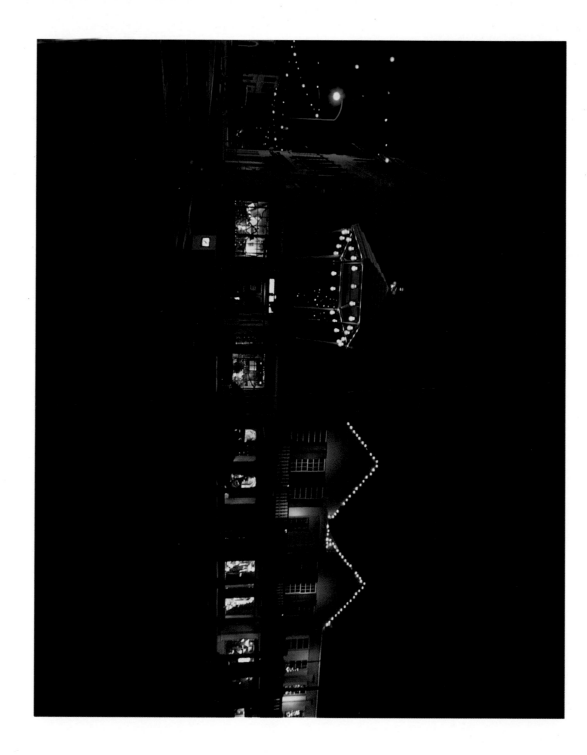

The "Birdcage", in Christmas splendour, Front Street, City of Hamilton

The old administrative headquarters of The Dockyard, with the twin towers showing time and tide

Junior sailors spotlit by the sun, Hamilton Harbour, Paget

Early morning light silhouettes Dalkeith, Stokes Point, St George

Ominous cloud formation blots out the sun, South Shore, Warwick

Windsurfer heads out to sea, Somerset

An old Bermuda dinghy, restored and awaiting a good pair of oars

A fisherman cuts through the early morning calm in search of bait, Ferry Reach, St George

96

Looking out from within the cave on Windsor Beach, Tucker's Town

The distinctive architecture of the John S. Darrell Building, Front Street, City of Hamilton

Camden, in the Botanical Gardens, was once the home of the Tucker family, and now is the official residence of the Premier of Bermuda

The baygrape sprouts new leaves in spring

A lizard suns itself on a night-blooming cereus

A unique hybrid of the garden hibiscus

Glassy calm water along the shoreline reflects the pastel pink houses

Traditional Bermudian architecture, at The Reefs, Christian Bay, Southampton

The *Fleurtje* alongside Penno's Wharf, St George

Pilings for the cruise ships, St George's Harbour

The night-blooming cereus; normally the flower will close and die by sunrise

Working the land, Smith's Parish

Transparent turquoise water along the North Shore

An unusual gravestone from 1889 in the Royal Naval Cemetery, Ireland Island, Sandys

The Easter lily field at the Perfume Factory near the Bailey's Bay post office

Hollywood Beach and the boathouse, Wreck Hill Estate, Sandys

A black cat stands beside freshly-picked carrots, at the J and J Produce stand, South Shore, Smith's

Full moon over Gibb's Hill Lighthouse, Christmastime

The north roundabout, Foot of the Lane, Paget

Johnny Barnes greeting city commuters on the roundabout, with Tamarisk Hall in the background, Paget

Walter Thompson, a gentleman of St George, with his friend Tiki

Mother sparrow and young

House signs on a quiet East End road

Horse and buggy on South Road in Southampton

Sunrise over Mullet Bay, St George

Honey-bee in search of nectar from a trumpet honeysuckle

The Hamilton ferry pulling in to the Belmont ferry stop

Mid Ocean Beach looking east toward Natural Arches, Tucker's Town

The old town of St George and its harbour, seen from Barrack Hill. St George was the original capital of Bermuda until January 1815, when the seat of government moved to the City of Hamilton

Long House, Water Street, St George

First morning light catches the morning glory

The Old Rectory behind St Peter's Church, on Broad Alley in St George, was built at the beginning of the 18th century and now serves as a library

The town of St George, with the rusted remains of the Swedish square-rigger *Taifun*.
Originally painted light grey and loaded with chalk, she suffered hurricane-related damage
in the late 1920s and was left to rest in her present position

Lone windsurfer sails through the sparkling sea off Sandys

Glen Duror, originally a harbourside movie theater, now converted to a comfortable home looking out across St George's Harbour

Somers Playhouse, the old movie theatre in St George, where many Bermudians first saw the classics of the screen

Dalkeith, Stokes Point Road, St George, the stately home of Lieutenant-Colonel Brownlow Tucker and Mrs Tucker

Classic Bermuda-style chimney seen against the waters of Christian Bay, Southampton

A little help on the playground; morning recess at Saltus Cavendish School in Devonshire

Saltus schoolboys in winter uniform, Saltus Cavendish

A fishing boat crosses the path of the setting sun in late summer

Profile of a functional Bermuda roof

Sunrise turns Ely's Harbour to liquid gold

Sunset framed in foliage on Wreck Bay, Sandys

The sun meets the horizon off Wreck Bay and Gunpoint Island

White Hall, St George, home of past mayors of St George, and of the Outerbridge family

Overlook, Harbour Road, Paget; a gracious turn-of-the-century home overlooking the City of Hamilton and the harbour

A colourful flowerbed borders the footpath at Wreck Hill Estate, Sandys

Red oleander sets off the crisp white brilliance of Come Aboard, a garden cottage on the harbour, St George

Traditional English herb garden, Sandys

Red oleander sets off the crisp white brilliance of Come Aboard, a garden cottage on the harbour, St George

Traditional English herb garden, Sandys

Enjoying the reefs at Warwick Long Bay

A pleasure boat cuts through the calm of Bermuda's North Shore

Trail horses cross the sands of Horseshoe Beach

The Belmont ferry stop, Harbour Road, Warwick

155

A tall dead cedar reaches toward the chimney of Dover House, South Shore

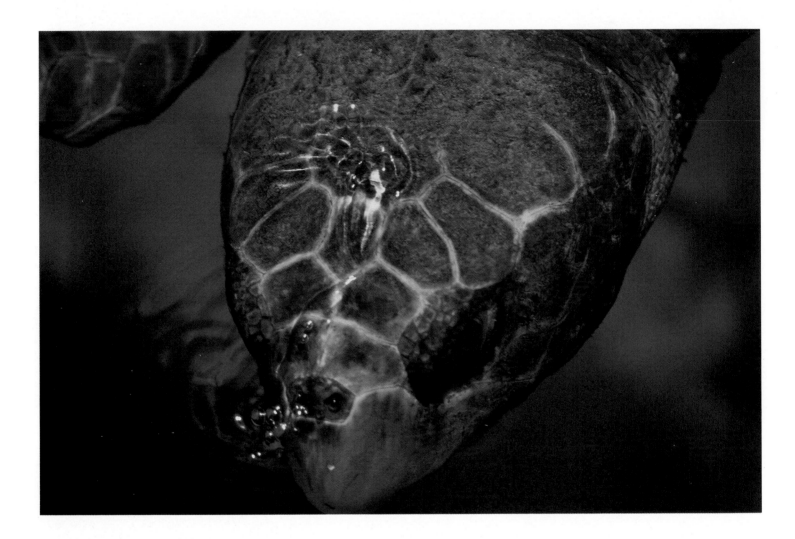

A loggerhead turtle breaks the surface for air, Sandys

Kayaking the waves at Windsor Beach, Tucker's Town, St George

Sky, sandstone, soil, sand and sea

Shelley Bascombe, former 'Miss Bermuda', relaxes in the warm waters of South Shore

International executive arrives for an early meeting, Civil Air Terminal, St George

King's Square, St George

Dramatic clouds at sunset over the golf course, St George

Light breaks through after a late afternoon storm

Setting sun behind the Sessions House and the Anglican Cathedral of Bermuda, in the City of Hamilton

In the damp air of dawn, a first gold glimpse of the newly returning sun is mirrored in an antique window-pane. Bermuda greets another day.

Palms

# ABOUT THE PHOTOGRAPHS

For those who are interested in the technical aspects of photography, such as film, equipment, lighting and exposure, I would like to provide some information as it relates to the photographs in the book.

In 1985 when I began shooting the images for this book, my choice of film was Kodachrome 64 and 25, but as I experimented with other film, I found myself using Fujichrome 50 and 100 almost exclusively. The colour saturation, especially of reds and greens, was noticeably stronger, lending itself well to colour daylight photography in Bermuda. Another important factor has been that the E-6 film processing can be done in one day at Bermuda Photo-Craftsmen.

The Camera I have made the most use of has been the Nikon F3 with the MD4 motordrive. A professional model, with the widest range of lens choice available, it is extremely durable and is backed up by excellent parts and servicing. The motor drive allows more time to concentrate on focus, composition and exposure, with less risk of missing a great shot.

Other cameras used were the Nikon FM 2, Nikon 8008 Auto Focus, Nikonos V in wet weather or shots taken from the water, and the Widelux F-7 panoramic camera.

The lenses I used primarily were: 24 mm F 2.8 Nikkor, 55 mm F 2.8 Macro Nikkor, 135 mm F 2 Nikkor, 105 mm F 2.5 Nikkor PC, 200 mm F 4 Nikkor Q, 300 mm F 4.5 Nikkor H, 500 mm F 8 Mirror Nikkor, 35 - 105 mm F 3.5 Nikkor, and 75 - 210 mm F4 E Series.

Over 10,000 slides were shot but were cut down to approximately 2,000 after the first editing, to 350 on the second, and finally 166 were chosen for the book.

The only filter used beside the UV lens protector was a polarizing filter which created the first image in the book and was used in other shots to cut glare from the water, saturate colours and create deeper blue sky for contrast.

The only filter used beside the UV lens protector was a polarizing filter which created the first image in the book and was used in other shots to cut glare from the water, saturate colours and create deeper blue sky for contrast.

On the few occasions I used tripods, the Gitzo Mono Pod was used on long lenses and a Bilora Stat IV with fluid head for the camera. However recently I found the Slik 212 AF with trigger grip and quick release to be most useful.

The advantage I had in shooting over a period of years is that I was able to capture the variations in light between winter and summer, the flowering plants in season, and the richer greener landscapes that I had missed the year before.

The majority of photographs were shot either in the early morning light or late afternoon. I much prefer the sunrise light on scenic shots and the sunset warmth for photographing people.

An important factor in capturing images that are unique is always having a camera with you, loaded and ready to shoot. This is difficult for obvious reasons, but the rewards are well worth any inconvenience. Keep the shutter speed on automatic and the aperture on F 5.6 for shots that give you only seconds to pull off. The metering system tends to be very accurate in today's cameras, which I take full advantage of in a rushed situation.

SCOTT STALLARD
St George

# ABOUT THE AUTHOR

SCOTT STALLARD was born in Bermuda 33 years ago, attending school in Bermuda, England and the United States. He graduated with a Bachelor of Science degree from Springfield College in 1980. Since then he has found himself in the hotel industry, airline industry, an actor and professional model in New York City, an assistant to a film producer and a health club owner, but without a doubt his prime interest has been photography.

A self-taught photographer, Scott is known locally for his fashion spreads for *The Bermudian* magazine's annual swimsuit issue and Benetton ads. His work has produced numerous magazine covers and sells as stock in New York City. Scott's photographs have been exhibited in the Annual Amateur Photographic Exhibition, winning first place for colour. His photos earned two first prizes in the Department of Tourism's photographic competition.

Scott's first private showing of 42 original works, held at the Bermuda Aquarium and hosted by film producer Robert Stigwood, sold out in a few hours. He went on to produce over one hundred other prints for collectors of photographic art. More recently Scott's work has been exhibited at the "Bermuda Contemporary Photographers" show during Heritage Weeks.

Scott's photography mirrors his concern for environmental preservation. His interests in this area also extend beyond the shores of his home to future projects on endangered wildlife, rainforests and tribes. Scott is a member of the National Geographic Society, Bermuda National Trust, Bermuda Biological Station, Bermuda Aquarium Museum and Zoo, the Bluebird Society, St George Historical Society and the Heritage Advisory Committee.